MW00564252

BOB CARLISLE
Butterfly Kisses
(S h a d e s   O f   G r a c e)

Transcribed by
Ted Wilson

CONTENTS

On My Way to Paradise

Words and Music by
BOB CARLISLE and RANDY THOMAS

Butterfly Kisses

Words and Music by
BOB CARLISLE and RANDY THOMAS

TO DOUBLE CODA

some-thing right to de-serve a hug ev-'ry morn - ing, and her

TO CODA

but-ter-fly kiss-es at night.

2. Sweet six - teen to - day, she's

look-ing like her mom - ma a lit - tle more ev - 'ry day.

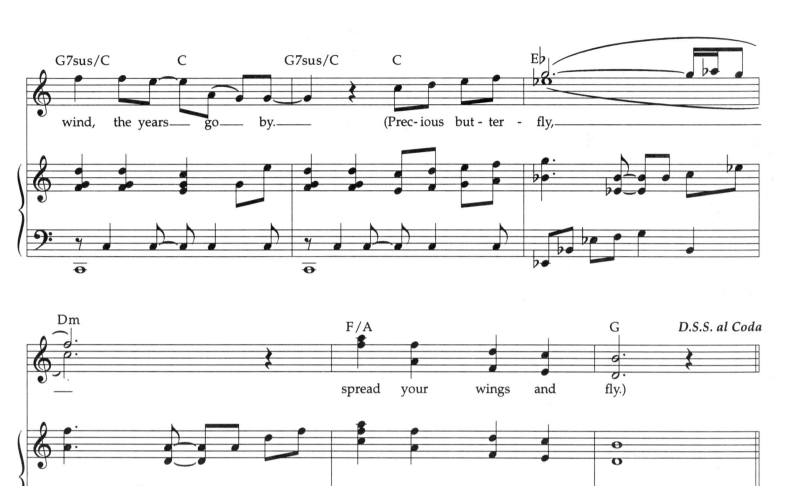

I'm Gonna Be Ready

Words and Music by
BOB CARLISLE and REGIE HAMM

Philly Soul feel (♩ = 92)

Oh,_____ and I'll do an - y - thing,_____ I'll do

an - y - thing,___ I'll do an - y - thing.___

Yes, I'm gon - na be read - y, I wan - na be a -

- ble to an - swer your ev - e - ry_____ call, Oh,

Living Water

Words and Music by
BOB CARLISLE and RANDY THOMAS

1. I feel your touch, __ __ I can feel your heart__ as I'm
2. Lord, so man-y times You've called my name,__ and I've

ly-ing here__ a - lone in the dark. I hear your voice
turned my face__ the oth - er way. __ Yet be - fore I e - ven

One Man Revival

Words and Music by
BOB CARLISLE and RANDY THOMAS

32

You Must Have Been an Angel

Words and Music by
BOB CARLISLE and RICK ELIAS

40

Man of His Word

Words and Music by
BOB CARLISLE, MIKE DEMUS and DENNIS PATTON

46

It Is Well With My Soul

Words and Music by
BOB CARLISLE

52 CODA

On My Knees

Words and Music by
BOB CARLISLE, REGIE HAMM and RICK ELIAS

Mighty Love

Words and Music by
BOB CARLISLE and REGIE HAMM

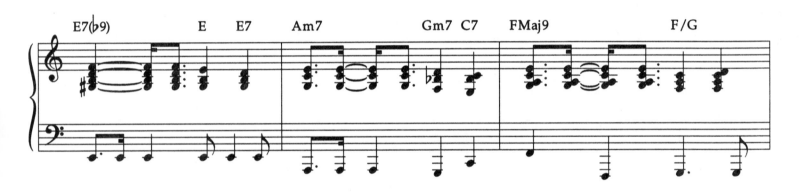

You should know me by now._____ I've al-ways been straight

66